MACULATUS

Follow Author Aaron Beitia

Instagram: @IAMKINGBEITIA

Books
Business Cards
Graphic Design
Logo Design
Custom Paintings
Graphic Prints
Custom threads
Custom Shoes
Photography
Body Painting
Event Bookings

For direct contact email Aaron Beitia:
Aaron.beitia@gmail.com

MACULATUS

—————————

Poetry By
Aaron Beitia

MACULATUS
Copyright © 2015 by Aaron Beitia

ISBN: **978-1519359971**

Edited by Ashley Rhame

Printed in USA

Dedication

This book of poetry is dedicated to my grandfather Alex Coleman Jr. & my mother Bridgette Coleman.

I thank you for instilling core values and life skills in me. They have prepared me to fly and this book is a token of my gratitude.

DEFINITION:
MACULATUS
Origin: Latin
\'ma-kye-let-us
Adjective
1: marked with spots: blotched
2: impure, besmirched

Introduction

"You are and always will be greater, than what you know."

I congratulate you for participating in this journey called MACULATUS. Your commitment to experiencing the most out of your life is priceless! For you to begin this transformational journey at this time in your life illustrates that you are now ready to take your life to the next level.

If you take the easy way in life, then you will have a hard life. But, if you work hard in life, then you will be able to live a lot easier. It requires us to believe it's possible to live our ideal life and taking action as though we believe.

This MACULATUS journey was designed to take you through my entire poetry literature journey from college sophomore year to graduation. The transformation that I've made has made me a more diverse artist and has really opened my eyes. The intuitive knowledge of understanding self is priority. This collection of poetry will inspire you to maximize your true potential. To get the most from this MACULATUS journey, you must travel with open eyes, open minds, and non-judgmental hearts.

Feel free to email your insights to MACULATUS@gmail.com so that we may celebrate your spiritual travels and victories with you.

Your life will never be the same. You will be inspired to make the most of your life.

Sophomore Year
Johnson C. Smith University
2012

New History

See, I've been thinking
On this long one passenger journey
Life represents revolving mirrors of us
Growth and development are relevant
Despite our imperfections and reflections
When the world falls on your shoulders
With no one by your side
Lift your head up
Look in the mirror
Ask who am I
Who are they to judge the life you live
Don't expect people to understand
God didn't give them your vision
My intuition is repetition
Looking down on the next generation
Full of degrading children and women
This is sickening
Injecting our young men and women
With mental health conditions
While all the men are locked up in prison
What more to say
This is more then a
Gasp of air they'll take away
This isn't just for black communities anymore
Now religion keeps us at war
What color are the janitors mopping floors
They laugh at us
 Giving up hope in our unity
Because you want to live filthy saying:
"Yo that wasn't even me"
When it's as true as can be
You want to go to college
But, you can't see past the TV

Your Worth

Hey! What's God's phone number
I want to let him know I called
Voicemail only gets you so far
I see past stars
Communicate over wavelengths
Through unseen barriers to relay this message:
"I have faith in everything that you do, if I lost everything and everyone I
ever loved I would still keep my faith because I love you"
See there's more to life then what we've seen
Spiritual realms are meant for souls
To connect so don't neglect
Better yet reflect and dissect your worth
It's more then you may ever know
Your value is worth more then gold

Fabric

Blinded by lies and greed
I bleed with a simple dagger
Brought to my knees
Never will I shatter
She smiles like always
Covered in mystery
Drenched in blood
Lost like New Orleans floods
I'm no thug
But, this bug keeps me itchin'
These laws are restricting me
Everywhere I go
Locs fall like a bumbaclot
Hands of the Father's clock
Lord forgive me
Time tales of a fairy tale
History witched spell
I stumbled and fell
Gather my thoughts
How to counter attack this plague
That rips our race apart

Peace of Mind

After piecing together shattered
Memories of past events that
Recreate future destinations is a
Cycling big wheel of childhood intellect
1 Corinthians 13:11
When I was a child
I spoke as a child
I understood as a child
I thought as a child
But, when I became a man
I put away childish things
So what's the purpose of imagination?
Ability of the mind to be creative
Through actions of forming
New ideas, or concepts of external objects
Not present to the senses
More then fancy lyrics
Modified beats and drums
That you can't formulate through nouns
Adjectives that translate verbs
Displaying actions
Invoking pure satisfaction
Can you imagine?

Lies

Lies are words in disguise
Sweet sensations
Illuminating Emotions
Covering up like Trojans
Walking through the front door
Like I've never looked into your eyes

Taking your essence as a present
Your presence is where I reside
Yes Lord,
I have sinned meditating
Over Kush and Corinthians

Elevated living art
Try not to get caught
In lies as I gaze in there eyes
Producing sweet nothings
Words that hurt
Habits that isn't easy to break
These are Lies

Praying to God

I pray God blesses me
With a beautiful woman
Who loves me for who I am
Not because she wants a baby
Or security of my last name
This is a game that everybody blames
It's a shame that it's life
Everybody isn't right
I need a backbone wife
She is more than just a ride or die
Plus when you make it to the top
It gets lonely and friends
Turn into unfamiliar faces
Leaving traces like cocaine residue
Genetics builds deeps
Instead of down and out
It builds cycles of plagues
Rotted fish and molded bread
Common sense to the census
It's relentless how we subtract
Brothers from sisters
Divide the remainders
No more family picture
Just American horror stories
You thought this wasn't a true story
Try walking down Wall Street
Literally burning money
The response is mental
The laws are invisible
The penalty is detrimental

Withdrawals

Peace and happiness
Is that too much to consider?
I'm a poet
An artist
A writer
An original thinker
Being able to create is natural
It's nature
I have this gift to give
With great power comes great responsibility
Then why is it that I feel alone?
Like a shadow mirror image of co-existence
Ripple effect of the cold hearts

Familiar white sound bounces off
Walls, ceilings, and floors
My worlds upside down
Frowns become common
Happiness of the one I love
Is know not enough
I couldn't provide it

She's better off
I feel as if I blew helium into my heart
Cut the line and traveled to another dimension
My loves so deep Vincent Van Gogh's
Ear couldn't compare to my pain
I would give you every organ needed to live
Without you I face death

My life and existence extracted through your eyes.
Damn and to think of lies
Manifested into ties
Tides me to the bible churches inscription
The creation of women

As Eve from Adam
You came from my rib, can you feel me

For one of my ribs is missing
For your love of forever in my system
I'm addicted having withdrawals of our love
Like an alcoholic in the liquor store
At the register living without repercussions
So what are dreams?

Lost One

All this work
I'm starting to feel like
The lost one on a journey
With no worries
Without companion
Starting to bore
Surely rushing is no use
Breathe, walk around, or smile
I'm back, stuck to you
Genetic codes embedded within DNA
Free falling in memory of love
Took my breath away
Your destination is a raffle
Lottery box ticket
Mathematician's digits
Computer coding, don't get addicted
Ticket to furnace gates and dungeons
This isn't Dragons tales or
Princesses held down by witches' spells
Snuff some snow they call it white
It's natural that's life; you'll be alright

All this work
I'm starting to feel lost
My ancestors fought
Found freedom in skies
Blew out candles
Still gimmie the light Jah rastafari
My roots lock tight
500+ years later
Great debaters morphing nouns and verbs
Into emotional avenues
City views down streets
White vans creep
Don't be another statistic of stained concrete

90 years and Running

Blessed before existence
This present didn't need gift-wrapping
Or perfect bow ties
This present captured unity
Family ties bound to love
Cherished memories
Photo snap shots
Threads of genetics made us
Each time I think about her love
I look up because
Big mama was always
A star shining bright
Each time she runs across my mind
I see her above
Generations built in her mold
Praise to God
For her beautiful soul
Big mama always said
"Let it be"
In hours of darkness
She is standing right in front of me
Speaking words of wisdom...
"Let it be"
When broken hearted people
Living in the world agree
There will be an answer....
"Let it be"
For though they may be parted
There is still a chance that they may see
So to those who knew she had that glimmer
In her eye and warm smiles
As she spoke into the world
"Let it be"
90 years and running
325 days
12 months
In the 12th month
The 25th day

The Lords presented to the world and our family
His angel, He blessed
A pair of wings for balance
One halo for wisdom
Family full of love
Big mama always knew
How to bring family together
The phrase goes
"Birds of the same feather flock together"
What's stronger; that's love
The genetic make up
Embedded code that creates generations
This deoxyribonucleic acid
Is mango juice for masses?
Invoking pure satisfaction
It doesn't stop here
So don't stop and stare
Continue with grace and elegance
Her presence forever near and dear
We may mourn for that we know
She has finally moved on
Like a good host
The celebration must go on
In celebration Jannie Mae Melton
Has gracefully moved on

When It All Falls Down

No one thought I'd make it
I'm suppose to be dead
My brothers and sisters are incarcerated
The control of a melanin painted people
It's easy to control poor people
Give money and take it back with interest
Eyes on the prize
But, what's the worth without reward
Mental block disorder
I mean mental black disorder
Society revolutionized
Codified as Slavery
See, the reflection in mirrors made me
Now, I see through eyes that visualize

I'm just thankful
God has patience
Graduating with loan debt up to my neck
For a piece of paper
To legitimize my intellect
I remember, when I thought
I never had anything
Yet, had to be reminded everything
I need lives inside of me
I need to learn how to bring it out of me

The more comfortable I get
You'll find out I like
Walking with your head in the sky
Rooted in Mother Nature like dew on grass
Before 7:10am sunrise
I remember 1+1=2
2 half's of a whole
Make since of daydreams in class exams
Snapping back to reality
How the fuck I'm supposed to pass

I learn technique of kiss ass teachers pet
One mindset
Two personalities
Two points of views
Persuasions a bitch

Creating what black people
Call a hook up
Maybe spitting good game
Like chicks named sunshine
Harlem night's pussy so good
You can throw it in the air
It'll turn into sunshine right before your eyes
They say it's breaking the law
What is the law until it happens?
Maybe it doesn't exist like
Children who have been spoon-fed
Bullshit and lies like
Christmas and thanksgiving
Please forgive me
I'm an artist
 I'm sensitive about my shit
But, when it comes to poetry
She's still like a new mistress
But, when it all falls
Who do you call?
What do you say?
Cause every body has there day

Junior Year
Johnson C. Smith University
2013

Black History Month

I make black history everyday
I don't need a month.
The ghettos will not magically disappear.

In fact, they will continue to grow
until the breaking point of a people's revolution

If we started from the bottom
Our foundation will be stronger then ever
As we excel upon dreams
And build skyscraper visions
That meet at heavens door

Black the color
The reference
The curse
The elixir

I break every little thing
I could get my soft delicate hands on.

They said I was a problem
A statistic!
To be silenced before I release havoc
Into the mainstream

After this mental slavery
Prison institutions of higher education,
Free student labor and dissatisfaction
Bombs break down monuments.

Bullets put great leaders to rest
But I still feel that bullet in my chest.
Marked with X
Is my last memory
As a king rehearsing
My own I have a dream speech

Running across war zones
Area 51 until it's all gone
Vague memories of what happened
And what use to be,
That meant the world to me
It captivates me
Intrigues my intellect

So that one day
My black people will rise.
Like the Phoenix out of its ashes
Reigns over the kingdom of The Lord
Father forgive me,

For I have sinned
Over a half a bottle of pinnacle
And slurred thoughts
Motor mechanics
Brain freezes

It wasn't wine but I could have done the same thing.
So, when I need to hear a song
That let's me know I'm strong
I can move on
The soothing vocals of black symphony relaxes me
For her words they remediate me and rehabilitate me

So that I can see clearly,
Lord,
God everyday is black history
Look at me
Twenty-two and no baby
Never been to jail
And I'll be damned for I can't fail
I can only move on to the next page
Where a new story resides

The author reads Black Ink Monks
Chapters are phases of life
But, the book of Samurai Haze
Intertwines life lessons wisdoms

And black ink that penetrates paper.

Substrates like a rapist in the night
Trying to get a nut off.
This is life,
My intellect is cocaine
My tongue is a razor
Take sniff, I guarantee you go insane
Into the lunar moon solstice
Break it down to its origin
Luna lunar lunatic

Greek Romans philosophers,
Homer and Aristotle spoke intellect
Learning from the Egyptians

So we started from the top
Somewhere along the line we dropped
But we shall never stop!

How Deep?

Can you Fathom a deeper personal emotion,
Which you simply can't understand?
To be... Or not to be
Black in America
Especially if you're not black
Rachel Dolezal
You know, NAACP
I identify as black
Damn, white people taking everything
The thought is scary
See, no seriously I understand
Why we look like menace to societies
If you cannot understand
What it means to be a tiger in a zoo
With a fake habitat
Then you will never understand
What it means to be black in America
This really bothers me
A black man with an education
Without the lack of enter detainment
Damn, my mamas proud of me
I got three eyes
Two to look
One to see

In lands of the blind
The one eyed man is king
But society plagues us with
Misinterpretations of selfish needs
Never perfect but always striving for perfection
Emotion, the human condition
Perfect is never quite perfect
Right... right?

We get pushed to the left
Feeling down about what isn't right
We must lift up

With our hands to the sky
March so our kids can stand
Define freedom
Act on liberation
Praise the Creator

Stay down like music to hearts
As it beats to the melody
Like unconditional love
Right mom?

She always kissed me on my cheek
Made me realize a woman like you
Is only half of me
But, me + plus you maximized =
      Our peak

Cancer

To much cancer
Not enough research
Plague society
See the demise
The government
Has done more than
Have you memorize lies

So, the revolution must be televised
Black and white
Is there really a difference?
If you dig long enough
You realize the hidden color
The value of pigment through fragments
Skipped like rocks on river beds
Throughout his story
History, wasn't meant for you and I
My brother and sisters that came to be
We are evidence of dominant society

We are living
On our ancestors prayers
Don't forget where you come from
History repeats itself
Malcolm and Martin failed

These higher institutions
Institutionalize,
Brainwash,
Force-feed us lies
African history doesn't start with slavery
Stop, please telling us lies

His story burned all documents
Chiseled all noses off monuments
As well as statues
They tried to re-revolutionize
Stop using your eye

See only truth
In sight
Only if your
In sight
Check it

Gandhi was a racist
Hated Kaffirs;
Niggers in a different dialect
Posted as a statue
In front of Martin Luther King memorials

May we have no peace?
Our only choice is to duck police
The life of black males
Are suppose to be in jail
So, why the hell should I give tithes
They say black people
Will only see heaven
After we rest in peace

Grandma been giving fifty dollars
To the church every Sunday
Yet, white man's heaven is on earth
The Asian man's heaven is on earth
The red man's heaven is on earth
The church makes 3 million every Sunday

The church invest in white banks
Bringing white entrepreneurs
White businessmen to buy all of the land
Force grandma on the streets
So, the church she tithing at
In a black community

Put her out on the streets
Too much cancer
Not enough research
And, if you ask me
Freedom was never free

Senior Year
Johnson C. Smith University
2014

What Is Success?

Ask yourself, what does success look like?

Where do you start?
These people, we people
Natural born leaders
Black people are million dollar markets

Ask yourself what does success look like
Is it doing right lawfully
Living by any means
Or is it doing what you love
But, what is love and does love bring success
The higher creator
Created and here I am blessed
Coming out of the womb was my success
The beginning journey of a personalized story
A success story; I've made it
As I live through days of my own movie
I am success
But, how does one acquire success?
You may ask
The answer!
Be blessed
Live with less stress
Smile more
Be great, you're blessed
The difference between
Normal and success is
An attitude test
Wake up with your attitude at 99%
Your gift presents 1% skill

Don't worry about money
Trust me
When the time comes
You'll know
So my question to you is

What does success look like?
Is it black or white?
Is it how you live?
Or what you wear?
Don't say life isn't fair
Life is what you make it
I was always told
Fake it until you make it
No too big
Not too small
Your hands hold the fate of us all
Kingdoms, leadership, and discipline
That's how we will survive
Stop listening to the media
And the government
They're force-feeding you lies
We are as great as can be
This journey will make
You and me
Hakuna Matata
No worries
Just let it be
Success is a mentality

Suicide

I never knew
The value of my life
After all the lies,
I visualize

All the robbing
Stealing
Killing

Open gashes
In my ear canal
Eternal bleeding

Rushed my body
Microorganisms overload
Eye vessels

Pumping blood
Until my brain Explodes

The decision
The choice
Man vs. man
Man vs. self
The choice
The decision

Gang or legacy
I could end it now
Let suicide get the best of me

While Women, weed, and weather
 Provide sympathy

Would anyone miss me?
What's all against me?

You nigger

Nappy head ass Negro
Cotton picker
Black
African
African American

Then there's the mulatto
My muse drank Moscato
Followed fantasies of twisted pleasures

My last day on earth
All but a swallow
I put the barrel to my membrane
They swore I was insane

It's your fault
Always been a problem

6-shooter handgun
5's the number of bullets in the chamber
4 lies I tell myself
3 times I replayed this in my head
2 my last thought
1 that started it all
0 exchange between hot lead

Penniless thoughts
Now my homie dead
But, like anyone it only takes but one
The ignition to the trigger
Were simply figures!

I'm an artist
At this time I painted,
My fragmented thoughts across walls
This is a public service announcement
This is what happens
When the world eats you alive

7 deadly sins

Pride

Belief in one's own abilities
 Interfering with individual's
 Recognizing the grace of God

Sit these who dwell in ignorance

Envy

Desires for others traits, status, and abilities
Please, those are called haters
They maybe right next to you
What's that saying?

Keep your enemies close
Your friends even closer

Gluttony

An inordinate desire
To consume more than one requires

Marijuana does that

Lust

Craving for pleasures of bodies

Lord, forgive me
I have sinned over this bottled brandy
She had me
Right where she was
It's pleasing
What a woman can do

Anger

Is manifested
In the individual who spurns

Love and opts instead for fury
But, I don't give a fuck
Right, Fuck you, you, and you

Greed

The desire of material
Wealth or gain

Cream; cash rules everything around me
Dollar, dollar bill y'all!

Sloth

You know the rest

My body declined
That of an escalator
Elevation dropped
    Ground levels
      Stone cold

My body as silent as the sounds
Eruptions between my corpses
Colliding with the ground
Newspaper turned it down...

Cultural Genocide

Can you see my eyes?
They shed tears
You call it scared

Eyes full of fear
Lifeless bodies
Hugged by quilted comforts
Brain matter on the ground
Paints a clear picture

Eyeless sockets full of fear
Can't see past the tears
Tears with every passing second
Grew heavier and more opaque
Threatening to overflow

Don't cry...
But, nobody was crying
It takes eyes to cry
We had no eyes,
Only tears where our
Eyes should have been

It's the dawn of new mornings
Yet these eyes are full of fear

Dig Deeper

Is it wrong to be an intellectual man?
Would it behoove you to pull up your pants?
See, this is how my mind perceives reality
Two lesbians, Smith and Wesson
Gets finger fucked until they nut
Formulating nouns climaxed into verbs
But aren't these just words....
Peer pressure brought me to a cliff
With a tree that produced strange fruit
Smith got introduced to Wesson
Crowds ducking underneath loud booms
Ears ring out without doubt
Screaming to god it'll be all right

These are just penniless thoughts
But, what's money without change
Companionship turns into blame games

Lame thoughts create petty drama
Little indigo children
Eager to become black men
Minus the education
For lack of enter detainment
Better-known entertainment of televised media
Instead of reading encyclopedias
Retaining knowledge and wisdom
They said; if you want to hide something from a NIGGA
Put it in a book, that binding has niggas shook
Love to see you fall
Hate to see you ball
Dig deep
Look in the mirror
That's the root of it all

I was born to win
Around sin and fornication
Patiently waiting 500 years
After all the blood sweat and tears

Now words are used like sheers
Cutting through material relatively similar to skin

Words piercing my flesh
Like hot rounds of Smith and Wesson
Yet, it is still a blessing
That tree of strange fruit
Better yet a territory, colony, island, or continent
Foreigners pick fruit like race picks color
Old money in the bloodline
As blood ties are closer then water
Our blood pumps 24K gold
Romans, Greeks, Europeans,
Philosophers, mathematicians, authors
Received teachings from Egyptians
The kingdom where knowledge was told
Behold 2560 BC dates beginning of an empire
Stop the riots and fires
Stop these hate crimes
That'll get you locked up
In 6 by 8 cells without bail
They told me dig deeper
We will make sure
To put you under the jails
Your tombstone reads cell
Your P.F.N is the
New P.I.N to capitol
Yet we go to school to get institutionalized

Love

You can predict it
But you can't prevent the weather
I'm just a gentle man
Looking at the way she treats me
You claim its puppy love
We say it's full blown
Like the king to the throne
You and me
Were meant to be
We have to make it work
People out here hurt you.
I don't need glasses to see truth
You got me lifted, shifted higher then the ceiling
You know that butterfly feeling!
I can't explain a game worth playing
But it's fair gain
Like good weed to the membrane.

She performs oral consolidation
Olympian tricks with her tongue
As she sucks and she spits
I'm stuck like the toilet bowl to it best friend
She is the shit!

I know is sick!
But, I want so much more of it
Not defined by love
But aware that our chemistry
Is met by likeminded qualities.
She wants a better me and I want the world
So I put on like my journey to the new world
Without order and communication.

What's a four-letter word have to do with it?

I mean nobody and I mean nobody
Can give me a definition.
It's a personal experience that has died

Before this generation
Now they are debating on strip teases
Music videos to find an exotic contemporary
To say "I love you".

But, I digress
Back to those perfect sets of double D size 40,
Perfect waist to booty ratio-
Out of this world!
I'm an adventurer and your temple has become my new playground
I desire to put my Indiana Jones Johnson in your temple of exotic
pleasure it's doom.

My shield is down yet,
I pray that you do not consume
Who I am into whom you want...

These are the thoughts
Running through my mind
Baby girl your as fine as wine
Mademoiselle I want to make real love
To your mental as we foreplay
Between thoughts of engaging interaction
You are my purest satisfaction,
All of this high with no drugs, no sidelines,
           or misconstrued thoughts.

Real love defined over time.
You will become my muse,
My Mona Lisa,
She was the goddess to De Vinci.
You are art to me.

What's Your Truth?

I want to swallow
Your natural juices
Into my vision
Straight from galaxies
Where she came
I made intergalactic love with her mind
Before I got to her body
When I got there
She was already
Wet…

Can you find truth?
In my lies
Or are these visions
Lies that keep
Truth unconscious
To the conscious mind

If making love is the journey
My sperm is DNA to life
I want to blow your brains out
Literally and figuratively
I will convert you
Conscious pleasure
Sapiosexual

I will open the passage
Leading to the Nile River
As I spread doors to eternal life

I will open your gates
With my tongue stroke
Make love to your second set of lips
Your beauty challenges me
As I quench my thirst
With your succulent juices
My tongue introducing itself
To your navel and my lips

Converse with your curves
Let's take our time, Ms. Cleopatra
I want you to scream
Until you are dry

Food for thought
Knife and spoon
I want to eat
Be my dinner plate
My eternal mate
Shifting into third gear
Beginning to shake
Your breast revolving circularly
You begin gasping for air

Your sweet spot
As delectable as can be filled my mouth
With forbidden fruit
That natural good good,
Not the artificial, producing cavities
Our bodies speaking foreign languages
As my lips make way to your mouth
Flavors sweeter than candy

We lose ourselves in chemistry
You push and I give you more
Than what you need
Your eyes searching for heavens
Looking back at me
Searching for the heavens
Looking back at me
Looking back at me
Searching for heavens
Calling on god

If this is pain
Pleasures not to far behind
Where would I be?
Tapping your sweet spot
Like my personal nuclear missile
The explosion producing

51

Juices and sweet nothings
Confronting real reasons
Why we are here
I feel your full of life
Warm creamy inside
On my dinner plate
Fellas can you relate
She wants to be great
Her personality is optimistic

A smile to die for
The look in your eyes sensual
Lustful, seductive, memorizing

Your touch
Your touch

Meditation
Rehabilitation
I want to taste all of you
From the crown of your head
To the souls of your feet,
I want to touch you
Please you
Rub you

Take a deep breathe
I want to explore these spiritual journeys
Through time travel
So that we can
Travel throughout history
Making love
Waking up from last nights leftovers
Stuck to my cheek and the pillow case

As we travel down pathways
I've never explored before
I want you to feel me
My fingers
My lips
The head of my penis

As it rubs against your clitoris
Igniting fireworks like clockwork
I want you to understand
That looking back at this journey
Last nights Netflix featured movies
You will be cum-ing
Harder than busted water pipes
Under busy traffic intersection
All we have is time
I want to master you
Like memorizing cheat codes in GTA V
My addiction is your temple

So I want you
To take every inch of me
Until your physical mold
Can bare no more
Then you snap back to reality
3:14pm last period high school
Came in your chair
See, wet dreams never
Played fair....

No Sober Thoughts

I seen you across the bar
The amaretto sour right

The way that you played
With that cherry
I was like "Oh shit!"
Don't you swallow it?

Now, let me tell
You my hypothesis

Life could be
A box of Chocolates
Something for something
That's the obvious
Now let me tell you something positive

If my tongue was a bullet
My mouth a semi-automatic machine gun
I would commit
187 homicide
Between your second set of lips
Tell me the first thing
That comes to mind

I feel free
As if I'm out my mind
I'm high
Don't pay attention to downsides

Is it true?
A woman looks at men
From his shoes
Then up
So within ten seconds
By the time our eyes meet
You already know
If you want to fuck or not

So, why did we meet?
She says, "You know what boy, you crazy"
Then I look at her and say
"To the tick tock and you don't stop!"
Cause I want to sex you up
To the tick tock
You don't stop

I've been picturing
You naked in a blanket
On a table saying, "Take it"
I could be your fantasy
You won't be dancing alone tonight

I can be your majesty
I think it's time
We take control
I got a place we can go
If you're down to go all the way
We can conquer the world
And no one else today
Be my partner in crime
Swerving through your galaxy

I want to take all of you
As bad as you want to give it
I want to give it to you
When your skin touches mine
I get goose bumps right away

You don't even know
I'm a fiend for your attention
I'm horny when you show it
So if you only knew
How I look at you

Call me crazy
Maybe we could be cool
I would…
Lick you in every direction

Lock you up in the crib
Just to fuck you...

All day!
I want to fuck you on the couch
Eat you in the hallway
Walk around naked

Put the cell phones away
Shadow dance for me
Until we find where we meet
Whenever you want to fuck
Just look at it and say "Babe"
So when that pussy gets soaked
We can call it today

I want to catch you on that liquor
Put it on your ass
Pin your little ass up
Fuck you like I'm mad
Finger you first

Make you want to fuck me bad
Soon as I fill that pussy
Step on the gas

I'm gone fuck you from the back
But, I'm gone do that last
So whenever you feel
That nut coming

You can fuck me fast
This is not just for the bed
I'm gone do you in the shower
This isn't a tease

We will fuck for hours
I want you to soak up the bed
So let's get a towel
Spontaneous shit

Let's make history
Let's get drunk in this bar
Expose every mystery
Oh shit, now I remember
No wonder
I recognized you
Weren't you my substitute teacher?
Back in high school

But I mean
Hey, I guess
MILF's need love too

Music Gets Me High

Once upon a time
I was a little boy
Finding my way on this journey

I call it
The midnight train
Do you want to know what I was thinking?

Sounds of retro funk
Give it to me
Give it to me

My third eye open
I can see clearly
Speaking foreign tongues

On and on
On and on

I got power in my words
But, my high is coming down
The world keeps turning on me
Oh, what a day!
Oh, what a day!

On and on
On and on

The day keeps going

On and on
On and on

Tell me what you know about this
Soul funk
Give it to me
Give it to me

The journey of life is all but a drug to me

It's for the "V"
Very, very extra ordinary
It keeps me going

On and on
On and on

I'm in love
As vibrant as
Jimi Hendrix electric guitar
1 for the money
2 for the show
3 getting ready
4 here we go
5 let me here you say

Music gets me high
Music gets me high
Let me here you say
Music gets me high

1 for the money
2 for the show
3 let's get ready
4 here we go
Music gets me high
High
High
High
Music gets me high

If I ruled the world
Black diamonds and pearls
I'd feed all my sons
If I ruled
If I ruled
If I ruled the world

I'd walk right up to the sun
I'd walk right up to the sun
See I'm just rocking right now
So all of y'all
Just rock with me
And let's vibe out

Music gets me high
Music gets me high

Graduation

I'm out in Charlotte this morning
Spain this evening
Complimentary the assets
Foreign Visions I'm seeing

College Graduate
It started to make sense

I'm an Artist
 And I'm sensitive about my shit!

I paint photography
I sketch graphics
I mold technology

And burn cause it's good for the soul
Labeled me a sell out
But I heard patience
Ain't nothing set in stone
Life is what you make it
Egyptian cotton my thread

The beginning of a well deserved weekend
That's how it is
When I come and go
Private first class
I'm trying to sum up my success
Without retorting to the past
That's called habits
Easy to catch
Hard to burn off

I'm great and I know that

So why people skipping steps
When it's a matter of time
Before they get knocked off

If you step wrong
Nowadays even titans
Can kill gods
You can get walked on like elephants

Either move
Or get stepped on

I got it
I'm on it

Did more damage
Then love did

Small faces gold bracelets

As I look around
Ain't much changed

But, I made it.

Goodbye

Just to get
A piece of mind

You have to do
Sometimes walk away

Hearing those words
You can't leave
Why wont you stay with me

Unintended emotions
Cold and alone

But detaching personal attachment
From reality will help you see things clearly

Like the birds and the bees
Play like children in the summer time

We all search for our
Personal contemporary naturally to me
World traveler and be free

It makes sense if money
Can produce change
Imagine water gives and takes life
Our pride possession with time ticking away

How many hours in a day
Failures translate into lessons

Teachers become subconscious
The withdrawal from reality is epic

Decisions come second
Emotions come third

Work in the morning
12:29am

Charlotte. North Carolina
Graduated college
An artist on the rise
Nothing is forever
I'm in pursuit of happiness
    I'm tired of hurt